D1400505

JOSEPH COHEN

ILLUSTRATED BY DEBRA SOLOMON

A Fireside Book   Published by Simon & Schuster
New York London Toronto Sydney Tokyo Singapore

I Love you
b e c a u s e . . .

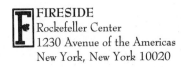

FIRESIDE
Rockefeller Center
1230 Avenue of the Americas
New York, New York 10020

This book is a work of fiction. Names, characters, places and incidents are either products of the author's imagination or are used fictitiously. Any resemblance to actual events or locales or persons, living or dead, is entirely coincidental.

Copyright © 1994 by Joseph Cohen and Debra Solomon

All rights reserved
including the right of reproduction
in whole or in part in any form.

FIRESIDE and colophon are registered trademarks of
Simon & Schuster Inc.

Designed by Bonni Leon
Manufactured in the United States of America

10   9   8   7   6   5   4   3   2   1

Library of Congress Cataloging-in-Publication Data
Cohen, Joseph (Joseph Edward), date.
I love you because—/ Joseph Cohen ; illustrated by Debra Solomon
p.   cm.
"A Fireside book."
1. Love—Humor. 2. American wit and humor, Pictorial.
I. Solomon, Debra. II. Title.
PN6231.L6C64   1994
741.5'973—dc20
ISBN 0-671-88229-5

*T*o:

*F*rom:

For those footprints next to mine in the sand.

J.C.

For my husband Alex: I love you because you've brought so much
sunshine into my life—I'll be tan forever!
And to Billy, the greatest bro on earth!

D.S.

Love

Such a little word. It fits on the tip of our pinkie. And it rolls off our tongue as effortlessly as a buttered pea. But behind its pipsqueak facade lies one of the mightiest words we know. A singular syllable luring us away on an endless roller-coaster adventure.

Love is silly. Love is sad. It's as grandiose as a rainbow over Versailles. And as no-nonsense as a frosty glass of milk. And so, when we think about someone very, very special, we think about *everything*. Dew-kissed cheeks. And bunioned toes. Silk pajamas. And a symphony of snores. Weekends by a rippling stream. And weekends mending leaky pipes.

And, on a good day, weaving through all the pieces of the puzzle, there's that wonderful spirit of *acceptance*. Adoring a person for all their strengths and all their quirks. And all their fabulous foibles in between.

Love. According to the latest rumors, it's going to be around for a long, long time. So keep it fresh. Keep it fun. Most important, don't keep it to yourself!

I love you because you're a sentimental fool.

I love you because you make everything look so easy.

I love you because you know all the best
public rest rooms.

I love you because you spoil me rotten
when I get sick.

I love you because you're so adorable
when you're kinky.

I love you because you turn

every trip into an adventure.

I love you because you're starting to look more and more like me.

I love you because you never step on my toes.

I love you because you never forget to say "God bless you" when I sneeze.

I love you because you finally threw out all your old underwear.

I love you because I always feel incredibly safe with you.

I love you because you always remind me not to stare.

I love you because my back loves you.

I love you because you're the only person who doesn't turn off the radio when I start singing.

I love you because you're constantly growing.

I love you because there's a giant deep inside.

I love you because you're the best secret keeper in the whole world.

I love you because you always see the bright side of life's cloudiest moments.

I love you because you never go anywhere
without a good book.

I love you because you've made room for me and all my baggage.

I love you because you don't make fun of me when I order stewed prunes.

I love you because you hate taking bubble baths
all by yourself.

I love you because you're even more compulsive about expiration dates than I am.

I love you because you're generous even when you're flat broke.

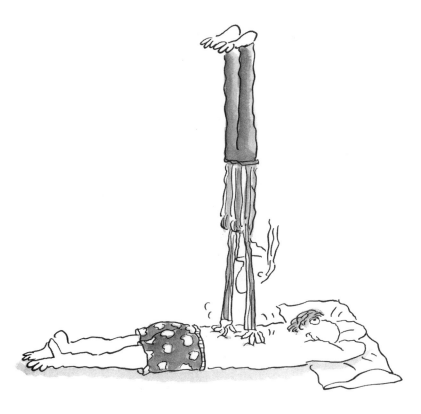

I love you because you give the most
unselfish massages.

I love you because you think there's nothing more beautiful than the beach in winter.

I love you because your hands are always warmer than mine.

I love you because you give me five minutes warning
before you lose your temper.

I love you because you have dimples
in the cutest places.

I love you because you warm up my side of the bed.

I love you because you almost always remember
to put down the toilet seat.

I love you because you never forget a name
at cocktail parties.

I love you because your skin smells like spring.

I love you because I still get a thrill watching you
take off your clothes.

I love you because you honestly believe you'll win the Publishers Clearing House sweepstakes.

I love you because you never confuse "between" with "among."

I love you because you adore the smell of hardware stores as much as I do.

I love you because you sneak cheap vodka into premium brand bottles.

I love you because you'll drop everything to cuddle.

I love you because you brush the dandruff off my shoulders.

I love you because the afternoon sun makes you
look warm and golden.

I love you because you have a knack for finding
the ripest pineapples.

I love you because your clothes fit me perfectly.

I love you because you make the silliest faces in front
of dressing room mirrors.

I love you because you never want to hurt
anybody else's feelings.

I love you because you get so excited when
I learn a new word.

I love you because you're the only one who understands my VCR.

I love you because life was pretty lonely without you.

I love you because you always know exactly
where to scratch.

I love you because you never let me
forget my vitamins.

I love you because you get more excited about Halloween than the kids do.

I love you because you're a million times
cozier than any pillow.

I love you because you make safe sex very sexy.

I love you because you love Ella Fitzgerald.

I love you because you always give me the first lick of ice cream.

I love you because you never stop trying.

I love you because you're the most patient bow-tie
teacher in the whole world.

I love you because you've turned napping
into a fine art.

I love you because you think BIG!

I love you because you're proud of me.

I love you because we fit together perfectly.

I ℒove you because

_____
_____
_____
_____
_____
_____

*L*ove you

because

$\mathcal{L}$ove you
because

_____
_____
_____
_____
_____
_____